Grade 3

Wake Up, Brain!! ™

300 Brain-Stretching Challenges
for Language Arts, Math, Geography and More...

Michelle Ball & Barbara Morris

ecs

These popular teacher resources and activity books are available from
ECS Learning Systems, Inc., for Grades K-6.

ECS1928	Get Writing!!™ Sentences	96pp.	Gr. K
ECS1936	Get Writing!!™ Sentences & Paragraphs	128pp.	Gr. 1
ECS1944	Get Writing!!™ Book 1: Sentences & Mechanical Control	128pp.	Gr. 2-3
ECS1952	Get Writing!!™ Book 2: Paragraphs & Forms of Writing	160pp.	Gr. 2-3
ECS1960	Get Writing!!™ Book 1: Main Ideas in Sentences	144pp.	Gr. 4-5
ECS1979	Get Writing!!™ Book 2: Main Ideas in Paragraphs	144pp.	Gr. 4-5
ECS1073	The Little Red Writing Book™	144pp.	Gr. 1-2
ECS1081	The Little Red Writing Book™	144pp.	Gr. 3-4
ECS109X	The Little Red Writing Book™	144pp.	Gr. 5-6
ECS1103	The Bright Blue Thinking Book™	144pp.	Gr. 1-2
ECS1111	The Bright Blue Thinking Book™	144pp.	Gr. 3-4
ECS1124	The Bright Blue Thinking Book™	144pp.	Gr. 5-6
ECS1790	Inkblots™	112pp.	Gr. K-3
ECS1804	Inkblots™	128pp.	Gr. 4-6
ECS9072	Writing Warm-Ups™	80pp.	Gr. K-6
ECS9455	Writing Warm-Ups™	80pp.	Gr. K-6
ECS9692	Springboards for Reading	96pp.	Gr. 3-6
ECS9471	Quick Thinking	80pp.	Gr. K-6
ECS1030	Math Whiz Kids™ at the Amusement Park	80pp.	Gr. 3-5
ECS1057	Math Whiz Kids™ at Home	80pp.	Gr. 3-5
ECS1065	Math Whiz Kids™ at the Mall	80pp.	Gr. 3-5
ECS1049	Math Whiz Kids™ at the Zoo	80pp.	Gr. 3-5
NU783XRH	Graphic Organizer Collection	144pp.	Gr. 3-12

To order, or for a complete catalog, write:

ECS Learning Systems, Inc.
P.O. Box 440
Bulverde, Texas 78163-0440

Web site: www.educyberstor.com
or contact your local school supply store.

Editor: Shirley J. Durst
Cover Design and Page Layout: Anh N. Le

ISBN 1-57022-226-6

Table of Contents

ECS Learning Systems, Inc.
Wake Up, Brain!! • Grade 3

About this Book

My inspiration for *Wake Up, Brain!!* came when I was challenged to keep track of the grammar, spelling, language, geography, and math concepts taught in my multi-age classroom. As an organizational tool, I created mini lesson plans for tracking curriculum elements for each grade or skill level. The plan included activities in five different curricular areas, plus one riddle.

My co-author, Barbara Morris, created a student- and teacher-friendly format on her computer. As time passed, we wrote more and more activities for grades 1, 2, and 3, and eventually created *Wake Up, Brain!!* for grades 4, 5, and 6, as well.

I use *Wake Up, Brain!!* as my daily mini lesson plan and expand the ideas in detail on the chalkboard or in class discussion. What a time-saver! No researching ideas or deciding what lessons to use. Students can finish all 5 activities and try to solve the riddle in as little as 5 to ten minutes.

Kids love *Wake Up, Brain!!*, too. I am constantly amazed and delighted at how practice with these mini-lessons enhances student learning in the individual subject areas. It only took a week or two for my students to get accustomed to reviewing the five subject areas at once. Now it's one of their favorite ways to learn!

Michelle Ball

ECS Learning Systems, Inc.

Each book in the Wake Up, Brain!! series covers the necessary elements for teaching grammar, language, spelling, geography, and math for a specific grade level. Whether you are a teacher in a traditional or multi-age classroom, a homeschooler, or a parent wanting to become more involved in your child's school work, *Wake Up, Brain!!* is for you.

Use *Wake Up, Brain!!* for—

✦ graded daily mini-lessons

✦ teacher-led or independent practice

✦ group practice

✦ assessment of student skills, including special needs

✦ reinforcement of essential concepts

✦ homework, extra credit, or quizzes

✦ acquainting parents with the basic curriculum

ECS Learning Systems, Inc.

Wake Up, Brain!!

Name: _____

Grammar

1. today i will use my sisters curlers and curl my hair

   _____

   _____

2. in February we are going to new york city new york

   _____

   _____

Spelling

Choose a word from this box to finish each sentence.

paste	enter	share	add	decide	fold

3. Will you help me _____ 33 and 64?

4. She will _____ her banana with me.

5. Which book did you _____ to read?

Language

6. Which two words have the same vowel sound?

   grow   cow   house   hot

7. Circle the words that would come between the guide words GRATEFUL and GREASY.

   grasshopper   great   graze   grease

   gratitude   gravity

Wake Up, Brain!!

Name: _____

Geography

1. You are facing to the north. What direction will you turn to go east?

   ☐ right   ☐ left

2. The Rocky Mountains are ? of the Mississippi River.

   ☐ east   ☐ west

Math

3. How many cups in a quart? _____

4. Divide each shape in half.

5. Why did the bubble gum cross the road?

   _____

   _____

Because it was stuck to the chicken's foot.

ECS Learning Systems, Inc.   *Wake Up, Brain!!* •

Wake Up, Brain!!

Name: _____

Grammar

1. lets read the poem my shadow together

   _____

   _____

2. i ain't going unless youll go with me

   _____

   _____

Spelling

Choose the correct spelling and write it.

3. where   whare   _____

4. downe   down   _____

5. over   ovar   _____

Language

Circle the correct past-tense verb in ( ).

6. Canoes (floated, float) on the river.

7. Children (learn, learned) important things at school.

8. The gardeners (plant, planted) flowers.

Wake Up, Brain!!

Name: _____

Geography

1. What state has four Great Lakes touching it?

    _____

2. What continent is cut almost in half by the equator?

    _____

Math

3. If the answer is 92 or 93, draw a triangle around the problem.

80	187	56	138
+ 12	− 100	+ 38	− 44

4. How many quarts in a gallon?

5. What happens when you throw a green rock in the Red Sea?

    _____

    _____

It sinks.

ECS Learning Systems, Inc.   *Wake Up, Brain!!* • Grade 3   9

Wake Up, Brain!!

Name: _____

Grammar

1. mr and mrs jones wanna know if i is coming with them

   _____

   _____

2. in art class i have drew to flowers before

   _____

   _____

Spelling

Circle the misspelled words in these sentences and write them correctly.

3. Blue is my favrite color. _____

4. I don't care at all for spinich. _____

5. This is Bill, my brothar. _____

Language

Circle the simple subject in these sentences.

6. The cars honked their horns over and over again.

7. My aunt sent me a birthday card two weeks late.

8. Lori's mother bought a hamburger for each of us.

10   **Wake Up, Brain!!** • Grade 3   ECS Learning Systems, Inc.

Wake Up, Brain!!

Name: _____

Geography

1. What two countries border the United States?

   _____

2. Which continent is south of Europe?

   _____

Math

3. How much money is this? _____

4. What is the difference between 17 and 8? _____

5. What weighs more: a pound of lead or a pound of feathers?

   _____

   _____

They both weigh the same.

ECS Learning Systems   *Wake Up, Brain!!* • Grade 3   11

Wake Up, Brain!!

Name: _____

Grammar

1. them girls taked my cousins book when they left

   _____

   _____

2. his friends havent no computer games to play

   _____

   _____

Spelling

Write the word with its correct spelling.

3. alwaes   always   _____

4. doesen't   doesn't   _____

5. float   flaot   _____

Language

Circle the pronouns in these sentences.

6. Fred went to the farm where he fed the horses.

7. The animals were hungry so they ate quickly.

8. She handed them some of her cookies.

Wake Up, Brain!!

Name: _____

Geography

1. What ocean surrounds Hawaii?

   _____

2. Which is larger: a sea, a lake, or an ocean?

   _____

Math

3. James has 6 pencils. Willy has 9. How many do they have together?

   _____

4. If you split James and Willy's pencils between three people, how many would each one have?

   _____

5. Why shouldn't you tell a secret to a pig?

   _____

   _____

Because he'll squeal.

ECS Learning Systems, Inc.

Wake Up, Brain!!

Name: _____

Grammar

1. someday im gonna have my own car

   _____

   _____

2. in April were going to phoenix arizona

   _____

   _____

Spelling

Choose the correct spelling and write the word.

3. teacher   teecher   _____

4. thot   thought   _____

5. more   moure   _____

Language

Check the box next to the word that can make the bolded word into a compound word.

6. **air**   ❏ copy   ❏ think   ❏ port

7. **cup**   ❏ plate   ❏ seed   ❏ cake

8. **basket** ❏ warm   ❏ ball   ❏ rake

14   **Wake Up, Brain!!** • Grade 3   ECS Learning Systems, Inc.

Wake Up, Brain!!

Name: _____

Geography

1. Which continent has the most land?

   _____

2. In what state is Los Angeles located?

   _____

Math

3. There are 18 puppies. Seven are given away. How many are left?

   _____

4. Sixteen frogs sit on a log. Six jump into the water. How many frogs are still on the log?

   _____

5. What time of day is the same spelled backward or forward?

   _____

   _____

Noon.

ECS Learning Systems, Inc.   *Wake Up, Brain!!* • Grade 3

Wake Up, Brain!!

Name: _____

Grammar

1. the girl had to borrow tom sawyer the book

   _____

   _____

2. there car it had hitted a tree

   _____

   _____

Spelling

Choose a word from the box and complete the sentences.

there	their	knew	new

3. I'm invited to _____ house for dinner.

4. This is my family's _____ car.

Language

Underline the simple subject of the sentence.

5. Kids stood in line for the carnival ride.

6. Trucks delivered big stacks of lumber.

7. Amy read a book about lizards.

Wake Up, Brain!!

Name: _____

Geography

1. Name two countries in North America.

   _____   _____

2. Color in which of these is NOT a city:

   ❏ Los Angeles   ❏ Iowa   ❏ Phoenix   ❏ Vermont

Math

3. Write the number that should come next.

   4   6   8   10   12   14   16   _____

4. What sign goes in the box?

   10 ⬚ 8 = 2

   10 ⬚ 4 = 14

5. What is a calf after it is six months old?

   _____

   _____

   Seven months old.

ECS Learning Systems, Inc.   *Wake Up, Brain!!* • Grade 3   17

Wake Up, Brain!!

Name: _____

Grammar

1. i and my friend have saw marching bands before

   _____

   _____

2. mrs glen lives at 3655 maple avenue in hartford connecticut

   _____

   _____

Spelling

Circle the misspelled words; then spell them correctly.

3. I no you are not going. _____

4. Mom helped us mak cookies. _____

5. I came in firste in the race. _____

Language

Underline the   predicate of the sentence.

6. We flew a kite in a field.

7. The old man fed the sheep in the barn.

8. The neighbors fixed the fence quickly.

Wake Up, Brain!!

Name: _____

Geography

1. Which state has a longer border on the Pacific Ocean: Oregon or Washington?

   _____

2. Which of the five Great Lakes is the farthest east?

   _____

Math

3. Angie had four yellow pencils and five red pencils. How many pencils did she have altogether?

   _____

4. Sam had three brothers and five sisters. How many more sisters does he have than brothers?

   _____

5. What 10-letter word starts with gas?

   _____

   _____

Automobile.

ECS Learning Systems, Inc.   *Wake Up, Brain!!* • Grade 3   19

Wake Up, Brain!!

Name: _____

Grammar

1. my sister said you done it on purpose

_____

_____

2. my watch says 1045 what does yours say

_____

_____

Spelling

Underline the misspelled words and then write them correctly.

3. The horse is my favorite annimal. _____

4. I have friends in Atlantic Citty. _____

5. Have you haad Mom's pie yet? _____

Language

Circle the root word of each bolded word.

6. **golden**   old   den   gold

7. **freedom**   free   dome   reed

8. **friendless**   end   friend   less

Wake Up, Brain!!

Name: _____

Geography

1. Of the 48 states that touch each other, what are the states farthest north and farthest south?

   _____

2. What is the only state bordered by two oceans?

   _____

Math

3. Dana bought a toy for $3.98. She paid for it with a five dollar bill. What change did she get back?

   _____

4. Gary needed three sticks of gum for every gift he made. He made 12 gifts. How many sticks of gum did he need?

   _____

5. What do you get if you cross an insect and a rabbit?

   _____

   _____

Bugs Bunny.

ECS Learning Systems, Inc.

Wake Up, Brain!!

Name: _____

Grammar

1. she dont like to go to burger king

   _____

   _____

2. mom said i am taking the bus to chicago

   _____

   _____

Spelling

Circle the misspelled words and spell them correctly.

3. You are my best freind. _____

4. I'm geting a bike for Christmas. _____

5. I don't know where I'm goig. _____

Language

Circle the word that has the same or almost the same meaning as the bolded word.

6. **wipe** the blackboard

   drive   wave   clean   write

7. **hammer** nails

   drill   bend   screw   pound

Wake Up, Brain!!

Name: _____

Geography

1. How many states are there in the United States?

   _____

2. What state is due north of Pennsylvania?

   _____

Math

3.
   $$258 - 169$$ $$77 - 58$$ $$286 - 17$$ $$13 - 9$$

4.
   $$13 + 2$$ $$17 + 90$$ $$871 + 117$$ $$127 + 98$$

5. How can you tell the difference between a can of chicken soup and a can of tomato soup?

   _____

   _____

Read the label.

Wake Up, Brain!!

Name: _____

Grammar

1. spot my dog eats a lot but he dont get fat

_____

_____

2. mr smith said you have drank to much pop

_____

_____

Spelling

Choose a word from the box to finish each sentence.

where	wear	made

3. I don't know what to _____.

4. She _____ a cake herself.

5. Mom, _____ is my coat?

Language

Read the sentences and underline the nouns.

6. The books fell off the shelf.

7. Carl and I watched a movie.

8. We didn't see any clowns.

Wake Up, Brain!!

Name: _____

Geography

1. Name two states that border Mexico.

   _____   _____

2. If you went to a home game for the Philadelphia Phillies, what state would you be in?

   _____

Math

Fill in the correct sign =, +, −.

3. 10 ☐ 6 = 4   4. 11 ☐ 9 = 2

5. 13 + 3 ☐ 16   6. 22 ☐ 3 = 25

7. Why did the kitten want to be a nurse?

   _____

   _____

She wanted to be a first aid kit.

ECS Learning Systems, Inc.

Wake Up, Brain!!

Name: _____

Grammar

1. zach was late because he dont know what time it was

   _____

   _____

2. me and nick we dont want no french fries

   _____

   _____

Spelling

Choose a word from the box to finish each sentence.

that's about didn't

3. I just want one, _____ all!

4. I _____ like his joke.

5. He knows a lot _____ dogs.

Language

Read the sentences and underline the simple verbs.

6. The girls played jump rope.

7. Fran used 30 stickers on her paper.

8. The dogs barked all night long.

ECS Learning Systems, Inc.

Wake Up, Brain!!

Name: _____

Geography

1. What is the capital city of Minnesota?

_____

2. Missouri is in what part of the United States?

☐ east   ☐ central   ☐ west

Math

3. The library sold 82 paperback books and 134 hard cover books. What was the total of the books sold?

119   216   52   182

4. Hannah needed three feet of ribbon for each of the five gifts she was making. How many feet of ribbon did she need?

20   17   15   6

5. What doesn't get any wetter no matter how much it rains?

_____

_____

The ocean.

ECS Learning Systems, Inc.

Wake Up, Brain!!

Name: _____

Grammar

1. i ain't surprised there team won the match.

   _____

   _____

2. that is the worstest movie i have ever seed in my life!

   _____

   _____

Spelling

Choose a word from the box to finish each sentence. | have   mail   people |

3. Put a stamp on the _____.

4. Many _____ saw the movie.

5. Do you _____ a dollar?

Language

6. Check the box to show the correct capitalization and punctuation for the underlined part of this sentence.

   We have <u>no cookies the jar</u> is empty.

   ☐ no cookies. the jar

   ☐ no cookies The jar

   ☐ no cookies. The jar

ECS Learning Systems, Inc.

Wake Up, Brain!!

Name: _____

Geography

1. Does Mexico have more land than Canada?

   ❏ yes   ❏ no

2. Where does the Bering Sea touch the United States?

   _____

Math

3. Phil had 32 stickers. He gave seven to his best friend. How many stickers are left?

   19   24   38   25

4. There were 25 candy bars for sale at the theater. When the movie started, nine were left. How many were sold before the movie?

   22   7   16   13

5. When Dirty Dan finished taking his bath, what was still dirty?

   _____

   _____

The tub.

ECS Learning Systems, Inc.   *Wake Up, Brain!!* • Grade 3

Wake Up, Brain!!

Name: _____

Grammar

1. my brother doug is the bestest player on the team

   _____

   _____

2. lets make a reading group and read the doorbell rang

   _____

   _____

Spelling

Choose the correct spelling and write it.

3. agian   again   _____

4. could   coold   _____

5. threwe   threw   _____

6. world   wurld   _____

Language

7. Which is the correct way to write the date?

   ☐ May, 26 1999

   ☐ May 26, 1999

   ☐ May, 26, 1999

8. Underline the simple subject of this sentence.

   The Broncos won the Super Bowl this year.

Wake Up, Brain!!

Name: _____

Geography

1. If you are traveling from Mississippi to Georgia, which direction would you go?

   ☐ west   ☐ north   ☐ south   ☐ east

2. Most of Yellowstone National Park is located in Wyoming.

   ☐ True   ☐ False

Math

3. Which of these numbers would help estimate how much 79 minus 31 is? Round to the nearest 10.

   ☐ 70 and 40   ☐ 80 and 30   ☐ 70 and 30   ☐ 90 and 30

4. Fill in the missing number in this pattern.

   5   10   _____   20   25   30

5. What kind of bath can you take without water?

   _____

   _____

A sun bath.

ECS Learning Systems, Inc.

Wake Up, Brain!!

Name: _____

Grammar

1. were gonna have a lot of fun at shauns house on friday

   _____

   _____

2. why didnt they shut the door

   _____

   _____

Spelling

Write the correct word in the sentences.

3. too, two, to

   My _____ friends had _____ much _____ eat.

4. knew, new

   Do you think she _____ it was brand _____?

Language

Table of contents:

5. What page has information about rats? _____

6. Can you find out about bears in this book? _____

ECS Learning Systems, Inc.

Wake Up, Brain!!

Name: _____

Geography

1. If your best friend moved to Boston, what state would she be living in?

   _____

2. Where are the Badlands located?

   _____

Math

3. Circle the numbers that are greater than 440.

   274   301   450   567   187

4. Circle the numbers that are less than 332.

   274   301   450   567   187

5. What kind of apple has a short temper?

   _____

   _____

A crabapple.

ECS Learning Systems, Inc.

Wake Up, Brain!!

Name: _____

Grammar

1. them boys are too noisy.

   _____

   _____

2. have you ever hiked here and hided in that cave

   _____

   _____

Spelling

Write the correct word in the sentences.

3. (Your, You're) _____ going to a slumber party with _____ friends.

4. (There, They're, Their) _____ kids play over _____ until _____ tired.

Language

Circle the words with the same vowel sounds.

5. freeze   stamp   stand

6. hole   cot   road

7. black   tall   map

ECS Learning Systems, Inc.

Wake Up, Brain!!

Name: _____

Geography

1. What direction is the equator from the North Pole?

   _____

2. What state are the Dallas Cowboys from?

   _____

Math

3. Which number has a 2 in the hundreds place, a 6 in the ones place and a 4 in the tens place?

   642   246   426   4266

4. Katy was the 9th girl to go to the library. How many girls went before her?

   7   8   9   10

---

5. What word, if pronounced right, is wrong but, if pronounced wrong, is right?

   _____

   _____

Wrong.

ECS Learning Systems, Inc.   *Wake Up, Brain!!* • Grade 3   35

Wake Up, Brain!!

Name: _____

Grammar

1. can you please hand to papers two me

   _____

   _____

2. well get our presents from grandma on saturday

   _____

   _____

Spelling

3. Circle the misspelled words.

   Jane wantd to have a party at the zue. She invited evry freind she knew.

4. Write the misspelled words correctly.

Language

Circle the word that has more than one meaning and fits in both sentences.

5. Please _____ me your plate. Put your _____ in the coat sleeve.

   give   hand   throw

6. Winter is so _____. I have a bad _____ and a sore throat.

   chill   cold   fever

Wake Up, Brain!!

Name: _____

Geography

1. Where is Cape Canaveral located?

   _____

2. Name three states that border Canada.

   _____

Math

Circle the number that matches the word.

3. Eight	4	8	7	6
4. Seventeen	71	77	17	18
5. Sixty-four	64	234	64	16
6. One hundred two	201	102	103	100

---

7. How many animals of each kind did Moses take on the ark?

   _____

   _____

None. It was Noah.

ECS Learning Systems, Inc.   *Wake Up, Brain!!* • Grade 3

Wake Up, Brain!!

Name: _____

Grammar

1. we was going to give the books to patrick and them other kids

   _____

   _____

2. i have breaked the chairs leg again

   _____

   _____

Spelling

Write the words from the box that rhyme.

some	gym	found

3. clowned _____

4. gum _____

5. him _____

Language

Circle the antonym of the bolded word.

6. **healthy**   sick   lost   kind

7. **awake**   asleep   dark   shine

8. **tame**   small   wild   big

ECS Learning Systems, Inc.

Wake Up, Brain!!

Name: _____

Geography

1. What is the state capital of Texas?

   _____

2. If you traveled from Nebraska to Texas, what states would you drive through?

   _____

Math

Circle the **greatest** number in each line with red. Circle the **least** number with blue.

3. 16   22   78   32

4. 358   428   983   883

5. 299   309   489   298

6. How did Dad feel when he got a big bill from the electric company?

   _____

   _____

He was shocked.

ECS Learning Systems, Inc.   *Wake Up, Brain!!* • Grade 3

Wake Up, Brain!!

Name: _____

Grammar

1. stephanie and me are sharing a book about christopher columbus

_____

_____

2. my neighbor mr jones said to me get off my fence

_____

_____

Spelling

Choose which word is spelled correctly and write it.

3. played   playd   _____

4. scate   skate   _____

5. lets   let's   _____

Language

Make compound words from two words on each line.

6. fire   song   place   can   _____

7. news   was   lunch   paper   _____

8. oar   row   bear   boat   _____

Wake Up, Brain!!

Name: _____

Geography

1. What is the capital of Delaware?

   _____

2. What river flows along the border between Indiana and Kentucky?

   _____

Math

3. Most popular sport:

   _____

4. Least popular sport:

   _____

5. Votes for soccer:

   _____

6. What two sports got equal votes?

   _____

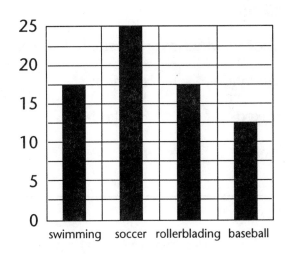

7. What goes up and down but doesn't move?

   _____

   _____

A staircase.

ECS Learning Systems, Inc.   *Wake Up, Brain!!* • Grade 3   41

Wake Up, Brain!!

Name: _____

Grammar

1. the movie starts at 7,30 and ends to hours later at 9,30

   _____

   _____

2. my sister brung me a bike that john borrowed me

   _____

   _____

Spelling

Choose which word is spelled correctly and write it.

3. everywon   everyone   _____

4. craked   cracked   _____

5. rane   rain   _____

Language

6. Underline the sentence that doesn't belong in the paragraph.

   The playground has a new piece of equipment. Every class voted for it.

   The parents helped put it up. I'm proud of my math grade. Now we can

   start working on another piece of equipment.

ECS Learning Systems, Inc.

Wake Up, Brain!!

Name: _____

Geography

1. What state would you be in if you were at a home game for the Miami Dolphins?

   _____

2. Name two states that border Nebraska.

   _____ _____

Math

3. Jennifer saved 236 pennies. Which is the same money?

   ☐ 2 dollar bills, 1 quarter, 2 pennies

   ☐ 1 dollar bill, 5 quarters, 11 pennies

   ☐ 8 quarters, 5 nickels, 9 pennies

4. What is 38 + 22? _____

5. Why did the man put cheese on his computer?

   _____

   _____

He wanted to feed his mouse.

ECS Learning Systems, Inc. *Wake Up, Brain!!* • Grade 3   43

Wake Up, Brain!!

Name: _____

Grammar

1. jeremy cant go swimming cuz he dont know how

   _____

   _____

2. my shoes dont fit since i growed so much

   _____

   _____

Spelling

3. Underline the misspelled words in this paragraph.

   Jane wanted to have a party at the zue. She invited every freind she knew. They were so exscited they jumped in the car and off they weant.

   Spell the words correctly. _____

   _____   _____

Language

4. Which sentences could NOT happen?

   ❏ Rain clouds filled the sky.

   ❏ The basket caught the ball.

   ❏ Lightning hit an oak tree.

   ❏ The bush walked away with my coat.

Wake Up, Brain!!

Name: _____

Geography

1. The imaginary line that circles the middle of the earth is the:

   ☐ equalizer   ☐ equator

2. A _____ is a small drawing of arrows that shows directions on a map.

Math

Write the words for these numbers:

3. 329 _____

4. 200 _____

5. 101 _____

6. What belongs to you but is used by others?

_____

_____

Your name.

ECS Learning Systems, Inc.   *Wake Up, Brain!!* • Grade 3

Wake Up, Brain!!

Name: _____

Grammar

1. the librarian finded my liberry card on the shelf by moby dick

   _____

   _____

2. the acrobat swinged on the trapeze way high above the ground

   _____

   _____

   _____

Spelling

3. Underline the misspelled words in this paragraph.

   The children used the phone to spread the news that there teacher wood be late for school. They didnt want anyone to cause trouble.

   Spell the words correctly. _____

   _____   _____

Language

Circle the word that tells what the bolded prefix or suffix means.

4. **un**happy   —   very   not   under

5. **re**read   —   before   clean   again

6. child**ish**   —   near   under   like

Wake Up, Brain!!

Name: _____

Geography

1. What map symbol is usually found next to the capital city of a state?

    ☐ an arrow   ☐ a star   ☐ a square

2. A large body of water that flows through land is called:

    ☐ a stream   ☐ an ocean   ☐ a river

Math

♡ ◇ ☐ ⌂ △ ☺

3. Color the 3ʳᵈ shape red and the 5ᵗʰ shape blue.

4. Underline every other shape.

5. The smiling face is the _____ shape.

6. What is produced in Brazil that no other country produces?

    _____

    _____

Brazilians.

ECS Learning Systems, Inc.

Wake Up, Brain!!

Name: _____

Grammar

1. tomorrow me and you can go fishing

   _____

   _____

2. dr jackson taked a bus to san francisco last Friday

   _____

   _____

Spelling

Choose a word from the word box to finish each sentence. | there   their   they're |

3. It was _____ idea, not mine.

4. Please set my book over _____ .

5. If _____ going, count me in, too.

Language

Read the sentences and write the verbs.

6. The books fell off the shelf. _____

7. Carl and I watched a movie. _____

8. We saw many clowns. _____

Wake Up, Brain!!

Name: _____

Geography

1. Name two states that border Vermont.

   _____   _____

2. If you went to a home game for the San Diego Padres, what state would you be in?

   _____

Math

Fill in the correct sign.

3.   14 [ ] 4 = 10   4.   21 [ ] 6 = 27

5. Circle the greatest number.   879   799   999   867

6. Why do firemen wear red suspenders?

   _____

   _____

To keep their pants up.

ECS Learning Systems, Inc.   *Wake Up, Brain!!* • Grade 3

Wake Up, Brain!!

Name: _____

Grammar

1. their doesnt seem to be enough ice cream in the freezer for everyone

   _____

   _____

2. were going to grandmas house for christmas well be home by tuesday

   _____

   _____

Spelling

3. Underline the misspelled words and write them correctly.

   Don and his sisster want to hav a garage sail tooday.

Language

Write the correct punctuation for each sentence. Tell whether the sentence is a question, statement, or exclamation.

4. Is this chair empty_____

5. That was the best hamburger ever _____

6. The dog is asleep on the sofa _____

7. Where is my soccer ball _____

ECS Learning Systems, Inc.

Wake Up, Brain!!

Name: _____

Geography

1. Circle which of these is not a state.

Utah   Chicago   Vermont   Texas

2. What is the state capital of Arkansas?

_____

Math

In what place is the **B** (b) in each of these words?

3. basket   _____

4. able   _____

5. keyboard   _____

6. What's the difference between a pear and a pearl?

_____

_____

The letter L.

Wake Up, Brain!!

Name: _____

Grammar

1. dont mr draper have to go to europe in april

   _____

   _____

2. he throwed the frisbee between ned and i

   _____

   _____

Spelling

Write the root word for each of these words.

3. golden _____

4. thinner _____

5. friendly _____

Language

Underline the simple subject of each sentence.

6. The bus delivers 34 children to the school's door.

7. The taxi cabs honked their horns loudly.

8. John read a big book about lizards.

ECS Learning Systems, Inc.

Wake Up, Brain!!

Name: _____

Geography

1. How many continents are there in the world?

   _____

2. Only a few plants grow in a very dry area called a:

   ❏ plateau   ❏ desert   ❏ edge

Math

How many all together?

3. ☐☐☐☐☐
   ☐☐☐☐☐   +   ☐☐☐☐☐   =   _____
   ☐☐☐☐

4. ◆◆◆◆◆◆
   ◆◆◆◆   −   ◆◆◆   =   _____

5. Why do we buy clothes?

   _____

   _____

Because we can't get them free.

ECS Learning Systems, Inc.   *Wake Up, Brain!!* • Grade 3

Wake Up, Brain!!

Name: _____

Grammar

1. I hided billy's baseball under the sofa

   _____

   _____

2. Hes going to mountain view junior high next year

   _____

   _____

Spelling

Circle the word that can be added to the bolded word to make a compound word.

3. **drum**   boat   bird   beat
4. **home**   door   work   foot
5. **sail**   bird   boat   drum

Language

6. Color the box next to the sentence about something that couldn't happen in real life.

   ❏ Soup was cooking in the pan.

   ❏ A tree walked by with a spoon.

   ❏ Aaron missed the basket.

ECS Learning Systems, Inc.

Wake Up, Brain!!

Name: _____

Geography

1. Name the earth's four oceans:

   _____   _____

   _____   _____

2. Which is usually larger?   ❏ a sea   ❏ an ocean

Math

Circle the greater number in each pair.

3. 116   161

4. 908   809

5. Write these numbers in order: 15   29   2   21   9   44

   _____

6. What always goes to sleep with shoes on?

   _____

   _____

A horse.

ECS Learning Systems, Inc.   *Wake Up, Brain!!* • Grade 3   55

Wake Up, Brain!!

Name: _____

Grammar

1. dear aunt mary cynthia and me would like to visit you this summer please write back sincerely jeremy

   _____

   _____

   _____

   _____

   _____

Spelling

Change these words by adding **ING** to them.

2. climb _____

3. come _____

4. read_____

Language

Birds	
Geese	2
Ducks	3
Robins	5
Woodpeckers	7
Heron	8
Seagull	9
Pelican	12

5. How many chapters in this book? _____

6. Where does it tell about seagulls? _____

7. Is this a good book to learn about swans?

   ❏ yes   ❏ no

ECS Learning Systems, Inc.

Wake Up, Brain!!

Name: _____

Geography

1. Which oceans border Europe?

   _____   _____

2. What country is on the southern border of the U.S.?

   _____

Math

3. Circle the numbers that are greater than 100.

   50   102   123   80   488   982

4. Count by five beginning with 10 and ending with 40.

   _____

---

5. What is the first thing you do every morning?

   _____

   _____

You wake up.

ECS Learning Systems, Inc.   *Wake Up, Brain!!* • Grade 3   57

Wake Up, Brain!!

Name: _____

Grammar

1. I have got no paper said brandon

   _____

   _____

2. tony and me rided on a big horse in topeka kansas

   _____

   _____

Spelling

Write a word that rhymes with the bolded word. The beginning letters will help you.

3. **clown**   fr_____

4. **tree**   fr_____

5. **blue**   gl_____

Language

Underline each word that needs a capital letter.

6. dick called to his son, benjamin, into the yard.

7. we watched a movie called *antz*!

8. mom and sharon went shopping at penny's.

ECS Learning Systems, Inc.

Wake Up, Brain!!

Name: _____

Geography

1. South America is a:

   ☐ country   ☐ continent   ☐ state

2. What state would you be in if you were at a home game of the Denver Broncos?

   _____

Math

3. Which numbers have a 6 in the ones place?

   ☐ 236   ☐ 642   ☐ 996   ☐ 321

4. Which number comes next in this pattern?

   25, 35, 45, 55 _____

5. 22 + 38 = _____

6. What has two hands and no arms?

   _____

   _____

A clock.

ECS Learning Systems, Inc.

Wake Up, Brain!!

Name: _____

Grammar

1. our group singed the song god bless america

   _____

   _____

   _____

2. we was going to caris house to feed her bird called winger

   _____

   _____

   _____

Spelling

Write the first four months of the year.

3. _____

4. _____

5. _____

6. _____

Language

Underline the simple predicate of each sentence.

7. The cat played with the ball of yarn.

8. The class recited the Pledge of Allegiance.

9. Jenny scored the winning basket for the game.

10. Many children lined the parade route.

ECS Learning Systems, Inc.

Wake Up, Brain!!

Name: _____

Geography

1. What ocean is north of Asia?

_____

2. What is the capital of Mississippi?

_____

3. The _____ Ocean is west of California.

Math

4. 7 X 2 = _____

5. 81 ÷ 9 = _____

6. Show 3:30 on this clock:

7. What do people make that you can't see?

_____

_____

Noise.

ECS Learning Systems, Inc.   *Wake Up, Brain!!* • Grade 3

Wake Up, Brain!!

Name: _____

Grammar

1. mathew and andrea were on one team jason and larry were on the other

   _____

   _____

2. the basketball hitted me on the back cried sarah

   _____

   _____

Spelling

Write the second four months of the year.

3. _____

4. _____

5. _____

6. _____

Language

Underline the simple subject of each sentence.

7. The cat played with the ball of yarn.

8. The class recited the Pledge of Allegiance.

9. Jenny scored the winning basket for the game.

10. Many children lined the parade route.

ECS Learning Systems, Inc.

Wake Up, Brain!!

Name: _____

Geography

1. Which of these state capitals is farthest south?

   ☐ Oklahoma City   ☐ Jackson

2. What is the capital of Arizona?

   _____

Math

3. 9 X 2 = _____

4. 64 ÷ 8 = _____

5. Show 11:30 on this clock:

6. What did one candle say to the other candle?

   _____

   _____

"Going out tonight?"

ECS Learning Systems, Inc.

Wake Up, Brain!!

Name: _____

Grammar

1. mrs bennett said we have been to south dakota this sumer where did you go

   _____

   _____

2. we were at the redwood national forest on july 4 1999

   _____

   _____

Spelling

Write the last four months of the year.

3. _____

4. _____

5. _____

6. _____

Language

Underline all of the nouns in each sentence.

7. The dog played with the bone.

8. The class sang a beautiful song.

9. Jake got the winning touchdown.

10. Fourteen children are home sick today.

ECS Learning Systems, Inc.

Wake Up, Brain!!

Name: _____

Geography

1. Which continent has more land?

    ☐ Asia   ☐ South America

2. Which lakes are NOT in the Great Lakes?

    ☐ Erie   ☐ Superior   ☐ Minnesota

    ☐ Michigan   ☐ Heron   ☐ Huron

Math

3. 200 + 350 = _____

4. 12 x 20 = _____

5. 333 − 229 = _____

6. What kind of table has no legs?

    _____

    _____

A multiplication table.

ECS Learning Systems, Inc.   *Wake Up, Brain!!* • Grade 3

Wake Up, Brain!!

Name: _____

Grammar

1. yesterday we writed a story i drawed a picture to go with it

   _____

   _____

2. my mom packed my lunch box with a sandwich chips and apple and a drink

   _____

   _____

Spelling

Write the correct spelling of these words.

3. break   braek   _____

4. bottel   bottle   _____

5. ribun   ribbon   _____

Language

Circle the words that need a capital letter.

6. The capital of oregon is salem.

7. My family is moving to topeka, kansas.

8. We'll be leaving friday at noon.

ECS Learning Systems, Inc.

Wake Up, Brain!!

Name: _____

Geography

1. Which of these states do NOT border Lake Erie?

   ❏ Michigan   ❏ Ohio   ❏ New Jersey   ❏ New York

2. The continent of _____ is nearly cut in half by the equator.

Math

3. Sally had a twenty-dollar bill and bought a backpack for $14.98. How much change did she get?

   ❏ $5.00   ❏ $5.02   ❏ $4.98   ❏ $4.02

4. Justin had 52 marbles. He bought 48 more. How many did he have all together?

   ❏ 200   ❏ 90   ❏ 16   ❏ 100

5. When is the moon the heaviest?

   _____

   _____

When it is full.

        ECS Learning Systems, Inc.

Wake Up, Brain!!

Name: _____

Grammar

1. Ive lost my january issue of mad magazine

   _____

   _____

2. my new address is 3598 jackson ave helena wyoming

   _____

   _____

Spelling

Which of these words are spelled correctly?

3. I like _____ bread.   ☐ wheet   ☐ wheat   ☐ weet   ☐ whete

4. Where are my _____ ?   ☐ shuze   ☐ shuz   ☐ shoes   ☐ shose

Language

5. Which of these sentences shows a mistake in the way the words are used?

   ☐ He left Ben and I at the door.

   ☐ We watched a basketball game.

   ☐ The doorbell rang twice.

   ☐ John will be late for school.

ECS Learning Systems, Inc.

Wake Up, Brain!!

Name: _____

Geography

1. Which is the largest?   ❏ ocean   ❏ sea   ❏ lake

2. Which is larger?   ❏ Texas   ❏ Louisiana

3. Which is smaller?   ❏ Delaware   ❏ Rhode Island

Math

4. Which number has a 5 in the tens place?

    ❏ 531   ❏ 205   ❏ 155   ❏ 315

5. Which number is greater than 6 but less than 13?

    ❏ 14   ❏ 5   ❏ 16   ❏ 8

6. Complete the pattern: 16, 13, 10, _____ , _____ , _____

7. What gives milk and has one horn?

    _____

    _____

A milk truck.

ECS Learning Systems, Inc.

Wake Up, Brain!!

Name: _____

Grammar

1. we runned around the hole playground for times

   _____

   _____

2. keith and erin doesnt like pickles i love them

   _____

   _____

Spelling

Which of these words are spelled correctly?

3. The blanket is _____.

   ❏ purpel   ❏ purpul   ❏ perple   ❏ purple

4. The person who took my coat is a _____.

   ❏ theef   ❏ theif   ❏ thief   ❏ thefe

Language

Which word has the **same** or **almost the same** meaning as the bolded word?

5. **carton**   ❏ shelf   ❏ box   ❏ movie

6. **tale**   ❏ end   ❏ fall   ❏ story

7. **gentle**   ❏ soft   ❏ breeze   ❏ easy

ECS Learning Systems, Inc.

Wake Up, Brain!!

Name: _____

Geography

1. Is the North Pole on a continent?   ☐ yes   ☐ no

2. Which state has the longest border on the Pacific Ocean?

   ☐ Oregon   ☐ California   ☐ Washington

Math

3. Draw a line from the figure to its matching word.

Triangle   Circle   Sphere   Square   Cylinder   Cube   Cone

---

4. What kind of water can't freeze?

_____

_____

Hot water.

ECS Learning Systems, Inc.

Wake Up, Brain!!

Name: _____

Grammar

1. were having a music party at ellens house at 600 p,m,

   _____

   _____

2. mrs jones has began to write a book called my years as a teacher

   _____

   _____

Spelling

3. Underline the misspelled words and write them correctly below.

   I went to the toy store to buy myself somthing with the money I earned. I accidentally knokt over a display of talking dolls. Evry one of them started talking at once!

   _____   _____   _____

Language

Which word is an antonym of the bolded word?

4. **damp**   ❏ dry   ❏ smooth   ❏ wet

5. **dim**   ❏ near   ❏ bright   ❏ dark

6. **over**   ❏ on   ❏ under   ❏ near

7. **gigantic**   ❏ magnify   ❏ small   ❏ huge

ECS Learning Systems, Inc.

Wake Up, Brain!!

Name: _____

Geography

1. What state is due north of Pennyslvania?

   _____

2. What is the capital city of Kentucky?

   _____

Math

3. How many all together?

   ●●●●●●●●●●●●   ●●●●●●●●●●●●
   ●●●●●●●●●●●●   ●●●●●●●●●●●●
   ●●●●●●●●●●●●   ●●●●●●●●●●●●
   ●●●●●●●●●●●●   ●●●●●●●●●●●●
   ●●●●●●●●●●●●   ●●●   _____

4. What is the difference between 65 and 60? _____

5. Why did the rooster cross the road?

   _____

   _____

To prove he wasn't a chicken.

ECS Learning Systems, Inc.   *Wake Up, Brain!!* • Grade 3   73

Wake Up, Brain!!

Name: _____

Grammar

1. Write your name and address as if you were sending yourself a letter.

_____

_____

_____

Spelling

2. Underline the misspelled words and write them correctly below.

   Jack isn't shelfish at all. He shared his lunch with me today because I was careles and forgot to bring mine. Now I know Jack is really thotful.

_____   _____   _____

Language

Which word gives the best meaning of the bolded prefix or suffix.

3. **un**seen   ❏ not   ❏ under   ❏ again

4. fool**ish**   ❏ can't   ❏ like   ❏ with

5. read**able**   ❏ can be   ❏ easy   ❏ like

---

74   Wake Up, Brain!! · Grade 3   ECS Learning Systems, Inc.

Wake Up, Brain!!

Name: _____

Geography

1. Which of these states does NOT border Mexico?

   ☐ Texas   ☐ Arizona   ☐ Oklahoma

2. What is the capital city of Illinois? _____

3. Which country has more land?   ☐ Canada   ☐ Mexico

Math

Write the number.

4. Seventy-four   _____

5. Nine hundred six   _____

6. One thousand two hundred fifty   _____

7. Sixty-eight   _____

8. What has teeth but no mouth?

_____

_____

A saw.

ECS Learning Systems, Inc.

Wake Up, Brain!!

Name: _____

Grammar

1. dear uncle douglas I will arrive in cinncinati at 430 on thursday cant wait to get there love ben

   _____

   _____

   _____

   _____

   _____

Spelling

Which spelling is correct?

2. Let's skate on _____.
   - ☐ Teusday
   - ☐ Tuesday

3. My cat is _____.
   - ☐ lazy
   - ☐ lazee

4. Our vacation is in _____.
   - ☐ Agaust
   - ☐ August

5. The door is _____.
   - ☐ locked
   - ☐ lokt

Language

Which word fits in both sentences?

6. The pig escaped form his _____. Please bring a red _____ to school tomorrow.
   - ☐ cage   ☐ pen   ☐ pencil

7. I read a _____ from my sister. I can't read a _____ of music.
   - ☐ paper   ☐ diary   ☐ note

ECS Learning Systems, Inc.

Wake Up, Brain!!

Name: _____

Geography

1. In what part of the United States is Missouri?

   ☐ north   ☐ south   ☐ central   ☐ east

2. Where does the Bering Sea touch a U.S. border?

   ☐ Hawaii   ☐ Alaska   ☐ Maine

3. You're in Georgia and headed to Mississippi. What direction will you go?

   ☐ north   ☐ south   ☐ west

Math

What time is it?

4. _____   5. _____

6. What time is it when the clock strikes 13?

_____

_____

Time to fix the clock.

ECS Learning Systems, Inc.   *Wake Up, Brain!!* • Grade 3

Wake Up, Brain!!

Name: _____

Grammar

1. I hope she dont break my new car said nick

   _____

   _____

2. we seen marys cat running down washington street

   _____

   _____

Spelling

3. Circle the letter or letters that make the "k" sound.

   crowd   keeper   rack   cost

4. Circle the letter or letters that make the "s" sound.

   decide   sentence   kiss   cost

Language

Which word best completes the sentence.

5. Tammy used blocks to _____ a tower.

   ☐ conduct   ☐ erase   ☐ construct

6. The storm made traveling _____.

   ☐ hazardous   ☐ damaged   ☐ grouching

ECS Learning Systems, Inc.

Wake Up, Brain!!

Name: _____

Geography

1. If you had a friend who lived in the capital city of Colorado, in what city would he or she live?

   _____

2. West Virginia is closer to the:

   ☐ Alantic Ocean   ☐ Pacific Ocean

Math

3. Write the fraction.

   _____   _____   _____   _____

4. What is the most valuable fish?

   _____

   _____

   Goldfish.

ECS Learning Systems, Inc.   *Wake Up, Brain!!* • Grade 3   79

Wake Up, Brain!!

Name: _____

Grammar

1. Jerry and me arent going to new york in february

   _____

   _____

2. mr baker said we have to draw a map of canada

   _____

   _____

Spelling

3. Underline the misspelled words. Then spell them correctly below.

   The cricket's song is the first one we here in the morning. The cricket cant actually sing. His songs are made when he rubs his legs together.

Language

4. A **simple predicate** in a sentence tells:

   ☐ who the sentence is about   ☐ what happened

5. Underline the simple predicate in these sentences.

   Jenny carried her puppy to the soft bed.

   Nichole stood with her hands to her sides.

Wake Up, Brain!!

Name: _____

Geography

1. If you had a friend who lived in the capital city of Tennessee, in what city would he or she live?

   _____

2. What state is Los Angeles in?

   _____

3. Mexico is in: ☐ North America   ☐ South America

Math

What time is it?

4. _____   5. _____   6. _____

7. What do you call a greasy chicken?

   _____

   _____

A slick chick.

ECS Learning Systems, Inc.   *Wake Up, Brain!!* • Grade 3

Wake Up, Brain!!

Name: _____

Grammar

1. lisa gived me a turtle names shelly said megan

   _____

   _____

2. dr. judy james taked out my tonsils

   _____

   _____

Spelling

careless	shy	thoughtful	neat

3. Change one letter to make a new word.

   why _____   near _____

4. Write the longer word that contains these letters.

   ought _____   are _____

Language

5. The **simple subject** in a sentence is:

   ☐ a naming word   ☐ a describing word

6. Underline the simple subject in these sentences.

   Jenny carried her puppy to the soft bed.

   Nicole stood with her hands to her sides.

ECS Learning Systems, Inc.

Wake Up, Brain!!

Name: _____

Geography

1. Where would you find a desert?   ☐ northern U.S.   ☐ southern U.S.

2. Which state has more land?   ☐ Louisiana   ☐ Vermont

3. Which lake is larger?   ☐ Lake Superior   ☐ Lake Erie

Math

4. Who read the most books?

   _____

5. Who read the least?

   _____

6. How many did Daniel read?

   _____

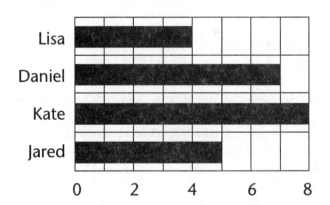

7. When is a man like a dog?

   _____

   _____

When he's a boxer.

ECS Learning Systems, Inc.

Wake Up, Brain!!

Name: _____

Grammar

1. grandpa peterson will be hear by 1230 will you be home then

   _____

   _____

2. can i take my new puppy to school ask donald

   _____

   _____

Spelling

| stir | clap | drag | hug | plan | grab |

3. Which word means *to put your arms around someone?* _____

4. Which word means *to mix with a spoon?* _____

5. Which word means *to take suddenly?* _____

Language

Which is the root word of the bolded word?

6. **fatter**   ❏ thin   ❏ fat   ❏ cold

7. **raised**   ❏ rise   ❏ raisin   ❏ raise

8. **happiness**   ❏ sad   ❏ greedy   ❏ happy

9. **fearless**   ❏ brave   ❏ funny   ❏ fear

Wake Up, Brain!!

Name: _____

Geography

1. What river forms the border between Indiana and Kentucky?

   _____

2. Which is closest to Canada?   ❑ Idaho   ❑ South Dakota   ❑ Oregon

3. All 50 states are north of the equator.   ❑ True   ❑ False

Math

What time will it be in 35 minutes?

4. _____   5. _____

6. Can you spell 80 in two letters?

   _____

   _____

A-1.

ECS Learning Systems, Inc.   *Wake Up, Brain!!* • Grade 3   85

Wake Up, Brain!!

Name: _____

Grammar

1. that book it isnt on the shelf like roger said it was

   _____

   _____

2. we dont got no maps of china

   _____

   _____

Spelling

3. Underline the misspelled words in this paragraph. Then spell them correctly below.

   Kenny is very polyte and always asks before he borrows things from me. He would never just grabb without asking. I'm glad Kenny dicided to be my friend.

Language

How does the prefix or suffix change the meaning of the root word?

4. **unhappy**   ❏ very happy   ❏ not happy

5. **beautiful**   ❏ full of beauty   ❏ no beauty

6. **reusable**   ❏ can use again   ❏ can't use again

7. **useless**   ❏ can be used   ❏ can't be used

ECS Learning Systems, Inc.

Wake Up, Brain!!

Name: _____

Geography

1. What major river flows into the Mississippi River just north of St. Louis, Missouri?

_____

2. Long Island is part of   ☐ New Jersey   ☐ New York

3. Which state has deserts?   ☐ Arizona   ☐ Alaska   ☐ Maine

Math

4. 2 cups = _____ pint

5. 2 pints = _____ quart

6. _____ pints = 1 gallon

7. What is a very hard subject?

_____

_____

The study of rocks.

    ECS Learning Systems, Inc.   *Wake Up, Brain!!* • Grade 3   87

Wake Up, Brain!!

Name: _____

Grammar

1. were moving to a new house the address is 9824 winding road tulsa oklahoma

   _____

   _____

2. will you please leave me go to the corner alone asked megan

   _____

   _____

Spelling

Which spelling is correct?

3. Rain made the _____ wet.   ☐ earthe   ☐ earth

4. He will _____ me how.   ☐ teach   ☐ teech

5. He's my best _____.   ☐ freidn   ☐ friend

Language

Which word is an antonym to the bolded word?

6. **tame**   ☐ wild   ☐ small   ☐ sweet   ☐ brown

7. **crooked**   ☐ clean   ☐ dirty   ☐ straight

8. **healthy**   ☐ love   ☐ sick   ☐ clean   ☐ green

9. **dark**   ☐ bright   ☐ light   ☐ night   ☐ kite

ECS Learning Systems, Inc.

Wake Up, Brain!!

Name: _____

Geography

1. What states border Florida on the north?

   _____   _____

2. What is the name of a group of lakes in the U.S.?

   ☐ Great Salt Lake   ☐ Great Lakes   ☐ Lake Great

Math

   What would you use to measure these things?

3. Weight: _____

4. Time: _____

5. Height: _____

6. What stays hot in the refrigerator?

   _____

   _____

Mustard.

ECS Learning Systems, Inc.   *Wake Up, Brain!!* • Grade 3

Wake Up, Brain!!

Name: _____

Grammar

1. homework tonight is page 32 for math chapter 13 for geography and reading jimmy and the boa constrictor

   _____

   _____

2. karen said she taked her piano lessons on tuesdays

   _____

   _____

Spelling

Write an antonym for these words.

3. young _____

4. left _____

5. nobody _____

Language

6. Underline the sentences that are fantasy.

   Tommy had a sandwich.

   The sandwich ate the chips.

   Rabbits hopped into the den.

   Wiley Coyote was hit by a truck and got right back up.

ECS Learning Systems, Inc.

Wake Up, Brain!!

Name: _____

Geography

1. Washington, D.C., is in the   ☐ eastern U.S.   ☐ western U.S.

2. Which is closer to the Arctic Ocean?   ☐ Africa   ☐ South America

3. What is the large island nation south of Florida?

        ☐ Hawaii   ☐ Cuba   ☐ the Bahamas

Math

4. Triangles have _____ sides and _____ angles.

5. Squares have _____ sides and _____ angles.

6. Name this shape.

_____

7. Why is the moon like a dollar?

_____

_____

It has 4 quarters.

       ECS Learning Systems, Inc.   *Wake Up, Brain!!* • Grade 3   91

Wake Up, Brain!!

Name: _____

Grammar

1. my mom growed tulips daffodils roses and weeds in her garden

   _____

   _____

2. for thanksgiving i wroted a poem called mr turkey and the pilgrims

   _____

   _____

Spelling

What does the **C** sound like in these words?

3	cave	☐ K	☐ S
4.	city	☐ K	☐ S
5.	become	☐ K	☐ S

Language

What punctuation marks make these sentences correct?

6. What a terrible storm this is   ☐ .   ☐ ?   ☐ !

7. May I borrow your math book   ☐ .   ☐ ?   ☐ !

8. Let's go swing in the back yard   ☐ .   ☐ ?   ☐ !

Wake Up, Brain!!

Name: _____

Geography

1. What state is made up of islands?   ☐ Alaska   ☐ Hawaii

2. ☐ True   ☐ False   The Atlantic Ocean is east of the U.S.

3. ☐ True   ☐ False   Washington, D.C., is in Washington state.

Math

4. Eighty-nine pineapples grew on the tree. Nineteen of them were ripe. How many were not ripe?

   _____ ☐ _____ = _____

5. One antelope ran for 92 miles. Another ran for 73 miles. How many more miles did the first antelope run?

   _____ ☐ _____ = _____

6. What did Napoleon become after his 39ᵗʰ birthday?

   _____

   _____

He turned 40.

ECS Learning Systems, Inc.

Wake Up, Brain!!

Name: _____

Grammar

1. there werent a single crayon leaved in the box

   _____

   _____

2. im sure that john was hitted on the head

   _____

   _____

Spelling

3. Circle any words in the word box that need **AN** as the article before the word.

bath	owl	foot	elf
girl	boy	shoe	book
oven	dress	egg	beach

Language

Circle the lines that have mistakes in the way words are used.

4. He wants to paint his wagon,

   but he don't got time.

5. Me and Mom let my little brother

   cross the street by himself.

ECS Learning Systems, Inc.

Wake Up, Brain!!

Name: _____

Geography

1. If you're at Lake Michigan, what direction is Lake Ontario?

   ☐ north   ☐ south   ☐ east   ☐ west

2. What river separates Texas from Mexico?

   _____

Math

What is the value?

3. 8 dimes, 3 nickels _____

4. 7 nickels, 38 pennies _____

5. 7 quarters, 2 dimes, 6 nickels _____

6. What insect can be spelled with just one letter?

   _____

   _____

A bee.

ECS Learning Systems, Inc.

Wake Up, Brain!!

Name: _____

Grammar

1. darla she taked her ballet lesson every thursday

   _____

   _____

2. aunt jenny invited us to her house for christmas eve dinner

   _____

   _____

Spelling

3. Circle the letters that make the **S** sound in these words.

   kiss   careless   ice   cost   fierce

4. Circle the letters that make the **K** sound in these words.

   black   poke   cook   kite   cake   cool

Language

Write 3 sentences: a question, a command, a statement.

5. Question: _____

6. Command: _____

7. Statement: _____

ECS Learning Systems, Inc.

Wake Up, Brain!!

Name: _____

Geography

1. Which continent has more land?   ☐ Europe   ☐ South America

2. The Arctic Ocean touches what 3 continents?

   _____   _____   _____

3. The capital of Maine is Augusta.   ☐ True   ☐ False

Math

4.   ☐☐☐☐☐☐☐☐☐   ☐☐☐☐☐☐☐☐☐
     ☐☐☐☐☐☐☐☐☐ + ☐☐☐☐☐☐☐☐☐ =
     ☐☐☐☐☐   ☐☐☐☐☐☐☐☐☐   _____

   Andrew has 20 pencils, Tessa has 25 and Jill has 15.

5. How many do they have altogether? _____

6. How many more does Andrew have than Jill? _____

7. Why did Batman go to the pet shop?

   _____

   _____

To buy a Robin.

ECS Learning Systems, Inc.

Wake Up, Brain!!

Name: _____

Grammar

1. mom buyed me a book called tom swift and the forest fire

   _____

   _____

2. aunt ruby gave jake and i an electric train for our birthday

   _____

   _____

Spelling

3. Circle the letters that make the **F** sound in these words.

   fuzzy   phone   if   enough   frankly   tough

4. Circle the letters that make the **G** sound in these words.

   junk   pledge   age   judge

Language

My brother woke up smiling this morning.

5. Who? _____

6. What? _____

7. When? _____

Wake Up, Brain!!

Name: _____

Geography

1. Does one inch equal one mile on all maps?

    ☐ Yes   ☐ No

2. What state has the longest border on the Gulf of Mexico?

    ☐ Florida   ☐ Texas

Math

Fill in the clock hands.

| 3. 7:30 | 4. 9:15 | 5. 1:45 | 6. 3:10 |

7. How do you make a lemon drop?

_____

_____

Hold it. Then let it go.

ECS Learning Systems, Inc.   *Wake Up, Brain!!* • Grade 3   99

Wake Up, Brain!!

Name: _____

Grammar

1. my lunch tray slided off the table

   _____

   _____

2. we havent no candy

   _____

   _____

Spelling

3. Unscramble these gardening words. Then write them in alphabetical order.

   sdees _____   _____

   krae   _____   _____

   truif _____   _____

Language

Add a verb to complete each sentence.

4. We _____ at the beach.

5. Each morning my dad _____.

6. I _____ to grandma's house.

Wake Up, Brain!!

Name: _____

Geography

1. A _____ is a drawing of the earth's surface.

2. Which is completely surrounded by land?

   ☐ a river   ☐ a lake   ☐ a sea

Math

Measure the lines and write the length in the box.

3. _____

4. _____

5. _____

6. What gets around everywhere?

   _____

   _____

ECS Learning Systems, Inc.

Wake Up, Brain!!

Name: _____

Grammar

1. yesterday was my appointment with dr johnson

   _____

   _____

2. where have you been

   _____

   _____

Spelling

Which word is spelled correctly?

3. ☐ grasse ☐ grass ☐ grase

4. ☐ house ☐ howse ☐ huose

5. ☐ twogether ☐ toogether ☐ together

Language

Write a homophone for the bolded words.

6. **their** _____

7. **bored** _____

8. **hare** _____

9. **eight** _____

ECS Learning Systems, Inc.

Wake Up, Brain!!

Name: _____

Geography

1. Draw a compass and place the four major directions.

Math

2. 328 – 207 = _____

3. 877 – 603 = _____

4. Sixteen monkeys found three bananas each. How many bananas were there all together?

   _____

5. How can you double your money?

   _____

   _____

Look at it in a mirror.

ECS Learning Systems, Inc.   *Wake Up, Brain!!* • Grade 3

Wake Up, Brain!!

Name: _____

Grammar

1. we was going to the library but we changded our minds

    _____

    _____

2. what is the best way too travel two hawaii

    _____

    _____

    _____

Spelling

3. Put these words in alphabetical order.

    grass   grain   grasp   grade   grant   gray

Language

4. Underline all words that need a capital letter.

    on july 19, 1995, a new hampshire social studies teacher was chosen to be

    the first private citizen to go into space. christa mcauliffe told americans

    her goal was to get students involved in america's space program.

Wake Up, Brain!!

Name: _____

Geography

1. Connect these uniquely shaped states to their names.

Texas   California   Idaho   Maine

Math

Color the shapes to show the fraction.

2. $^3/_4$

3. $^1/_2$

4. $^2/_3$

5. What has 50 heads and 50 tails?

_____

_____

Fifty pennies.

ECS Learning Systems, Inc.

Answer Key

Note: Grammar activities may occasionally have more than one possible answer.

Page 6
1. Today I will use my sister's curlers and curl my hair.
2. In February we are going to New York City, New York.
3. add
4. share
5. decide
6. house/cow
7. graze, grease, gratitude, gravity

Page 7
1. right
2. west
3. 4 cups
4. Each shape should be divided in half.

Page 8
1. Let's read the poem, "My Shadow," together.
2. I am not going unless you'll go with me.
3. where
4. down
5. over
6. floated
7. learned
8. planted

Page 9
1. Michigan
2. Africa
3. 80 +12
4. 4 quarts in a gallon

Page 10
1. Mr. and Mrs. Jones want to know if I am going with them.
2. In art class I drew two flowers before.
3. favorite
4. don't
5. brother
6. cars
7. aunt
8. mother

Page 11
1. Canada and Mexico
2. Africa

3. $1.30
4. 9

Page 12
1. Those girls took my cousin's book when they left.
2. His friends have no computer games to play.
3. always
4. doesn't
5. float
6. he
7. they
8. she, them, her

Page 13
1. Pacific Ocean
2. ocean
3. 15
4. 5

Page 14
1. Someday I'm going to have my own car.
2. In April we're going to Phoenix, Arizona.
3. teacher
4. thought
5. more
6. port
7. cake
8. ball

Page 15
1. Asia
2. California
3. 11
4. 10

Page 16
1. The girl has come to borrow <u>Tom Sawyer</u>, the book.
2. Their car hit a tree.
3. their
4. new
5. Kids
6. Trucks
7. Amy

Page 17
1. Mexico, Canada, U.S., Central American countries
2. Iowa, Vermont
3. 18
4. –, +

Page 18
1. My friend and I have seen marching bands before.
2. Mrs. Glen lives at 3665 Maple Avenue in Hartford, Connecticut.
3. know
4. make
5. first
6. flew
7. fed
8. fixed

Page 19
1. Oregon
2. Lake Ontario
3. 9
4. 2

Page 20
1. My sister said you did it on purpose.
2. My watch says 10:45. What does yours say?
3. animal
4. City
5. had
6. gold
7. free
8. friend

Page 21
1. Maine = north, and Florida = south
2. Alaska
3. $1.02
4. 36

Page 22
1. She doesn't like to go to Burger King.
2. Mom said I am taking the bus to Chicago.
3. friend
4. getting

ECS Learning Systems, Inc.

Answer Key

5. going
6. clean
7. pound

Page 23
1. 50
2. New York
3. 89, 19, 269, 4
4. 15, 107, 988, 225

Page 24
1. Spot, my dog, eats a lot, but he doesn't get fat.
2. Mrs. Smith said, "You drank too much pop."
3. wear
4. made
5. where
6. books, shelf
7. Carl, movie
8. clowns

Page 25
1. TX, NM, CA, or AZ
2. Pennsylvania
3. –
4. –
5. =
6. +

Page 26
1. Zack was late because he didn't know what time it was.
2. Nick and I don't want any french fries.
3. that's
4. didn't
5. about
6. played
7. used
8. barked

Page 27
1. Minneapolis
2. central
3. 216
4. 15

Page 28
1. I'm not surprised their team won the match.
2. That is the worst movie I have

ever seen in my life!
3. mail
4. people
5. have
6. no cookies. The jar

Page 29
1. No
2. Alaska
3. 25
4. 16

Page 30
1. My brother, Doug, is the best player on the team.
2. Let's make a reading group and read The Doorbell Rang.
3. again
4. could
5. threw
6. world
7. May 26, 1999
8. Broncos

Page 31
1. east
2. True
3. 80 and 30
4. 15

Page 32
1. We're going to have a lot of fun at Shaun's house on Friday.
2. Why didn't they shut the door?
3. two, too, to
4. knew, new
5. 7
6. No

Page 33
1. Massachusetts
2. South Dakota
3. 450, 567
4. 274, 301,187

Page 34
1. Those boys are too noisy.
2. Have you ever hiked here and hidden in that cave?
3. You're, Your

4. Their, there, they're
5. stamp/stand
6. hole/road
7. black/map

Page 35
1. South
2. Texas
3. 246
4. 8

Page 36
1. Can you please hand two papers to me?
2. We'll get our presents from Grandma on Saturday.
3/4. wanted, zoo, every, friend
5. hand
6. cold

Page 37
1. Florida
2. AK, WA, ID, MT, ND, MN, MI, NY, VT, NH or ME.
3. 8
4. 17
5. 64
6. 102

Page 38
1. We were going to give the books to Patrick and the other kids.
2. I have broken the chair's leg again.
3. found
4. some
5. gym
6. sick
7. asleep
8. wild

Page 39
1. Austin
2. Kansas and Oklahoma
3. 78 (red) 16 (blue)
4. 983 (red) 358 (blue)
5. 489 (red) 298 (blue)

Page 40
1. Stephanie and I are sharing a book about Christopher Columbus.

ECS Learning Systems, Inc.

Answer Key

2. My neighbor, Mr. Jones, said to me, "Get off my fence!"
3. played
4. skate
5. let's
6. fireplace
7. newspaper
8. rowboat

Page 41
1. Dover
2. Ohio River
3. soccer
4. baseball
5. 25
6. swimming, rollerblading

Page 42
1. The movie starts at 7:30 and ends two hours later at 9:30.
2. My sister brought me a bike that John loaned me.
3. everyone
4. cracked
5. rain
6. I'm proud of my math grade.

Page 43
1. Florida
2. SD, WY, CO, KA, MO or IA
3. 1 dollar bill, 5 quarters, 11 pennies
4. 60

Page 44
1. Jeremy can't go swimming because he doesn't know how.
2. My shoes don't fit since I grew so much.
3. zoo, friend, went
4. The basket caught the ball./The bush walked away with my coat.

Page 45
1. equator
2. compass
3. Three hundred twenty nine
4. Two hundred
5. One hundred one

Page 46
1. The librarian found my library card on the shelf by <u>Moby Dick</u>.
2. The acrobat swung on the trapeze high above the ground.
3. Their, would, didn't
4. not
5. again
6. like

Page 47
1. A star
2. river
3. square (red) triangle (blue)
4. Every other shape should be underlined.
5. 6th

Page 48
1. Tomorrow you and I can go fishing.
2. Dr. Jackson took a bus to San Francisco last Friday.
3. their
4. there
5. they're
6. fell
7. watched
8. saw

Page 49
1. NY, NH or MA
2. California
3. –
4. +
5. 999

Page 50
1. There doesn't seem to be enough ice cream in the freezer for everyone.
2. We're going to Grandma's house for Christmas. We'll be home by Tuesday.
3. sister, have, sale, today
4. ? Question
5. . or !
6. . Statement
7. ? Question

Page 51
1. Chicago
2. Little Rock

3. first
4. second
5. fourth

Page 52
1. Doesn't Mr. Draper have to go to Europe in April?
2. He threw the frisbee between Ned and me.
3. gold
4. thin
5. friend
6. bus
7. cabs
8. John

Page 53
1. 7
2. desert
3. 19
4. 7

Page 54
1. I hid Billy's baseball under the sofa.
2. He's going to Mountain View Junior High next year.
3. beat
4. work
5. boat
6. A tree walked by with a spoon.

Page 55
1. Atlantic, Pacific, Arctic, Indian
2. ocean
3. 161
4. 908
5. 2, 9, 15, 21, 29, 44

Page 56
1. Dear Aunt Mary,
   Cynthia and I would like to visit you this summer. Please write back.
   Sincerely,
   Jeremy
2. climbing
3. coming
4. reading
5. 7
6. page 9
7. no

108   Wake Up, Brain!! • Grade 3   ECS Learning Systems, Inc.

Answer Key

Page 57
1. Atlantic, Arctic
2. Mexico
3. 102, 123, 488, 982
4. 10, 15, 20, 25, 30, 35, 40

Page 58
1. "I have no paper," said Brandon.
2. Tony and I rode on a big horse in Topeka, Kansas.
3. frown
4. free
5. glue
6. Dick, Benjamin
7. We, *Antz*
8. Mom, Sharon, Penney's

Page 59
1. continent
2. Colorado
3. 236, 996
4. 65
5. 60

Page 60
1. Our group sang the song "God Bless America!"
2. We were going to Cari's house to feed her bird called Winger.
3. January
4. February
5. March
6. April
7. played
8. recited
9. scored
10. lined

Page 61
1. Arctic
2. Jackson
3. Pacific
4. 14
5. 9
6. Small hand on 3, big hand on 6.

Page 62
1. Matthew and Andrea were on one team. Jason and Larry were on the other.
2. "The basketball hit me on the back!" cried Sarah.

3. May
4. June
5. July
6. August
7. cat
8. class
9. Jenny
10. children

Page 63
1. Jackson
2. Phoenix
3. 18
4. 8
5. Small hand on 11, big hand on 6.

Page 64
1. Mrs. Bennett said, "We have been to South Dakota this summer. Where did you go?"
2. We were at the Redwood National Forest on July 4, 1999.
3. September
4. October
5. November
6. December
7. dog, bone
8. class, song
9. Jake, touchdown
10. children

Page 65
1. Asia
2. Minnesota, Heron
3. 550
4. 240
5. 104

Page 66
1. Yesterday we wrote a story. I drew a picture to go with it.
2. My mom packed my lunch box with a sandwich, chips, an apple, and a drink.
3. break
4. bottle
5. ribbon
6. Oregon, Salem
7. Topeka, Kansas
8. Friday

Page 67
1. New Jersey
2. Africa
3. $5.02
4. 100

Page 68
1. I've lost my January issue of <u>Mad Magazine</u>.
2. My new address is 3598 Jackson Avenue, Helena, Wyoming.
3. wheat
4. shoes
5. He left Ben and me at the door.

Page 69
1. ocean
2. Texas
3. Rhode Island
4. 155
5. 8
6. 7, 4, 1

Page 70
1. We ran around the whole playground four times.
2. Keith and Erin don't like pickles. I love them.
3. purple
4. thief
5. box
6. story
7. soft

Page 71
1. No (in the Arctic Ocean)
2. California
3. sphere, cone, circle, cylinder, square, triangle, cube

Page 72
1. We're having a music party at Ellen's house at 6:00 p.m.
2. Mrs. Jones has begun to write a book called <u>My Years as a Teacher</u>.
3. something, knocked, every
4. dry
5. bright
6. under
7. small

ECS Learning Systems, Inc.   *Wake Up, Brain!!* • Grade 3

Answer Key

Page 73
1. New York
2. Louisville
3. 91
4. 5

Page 74
1. Look for proper capitalization, punctuation, and format.
2. selfish, careless, thoughtful
3. not
4. like
5. can be

Page 75
1. Oklahoma
2. Springfield
3. Canada
4. 74
5. 906
6. 1,250
7. 68

Page 76
1. Dear Uncle Douglas,
   I will arrive in Cincinnati at 4:30 on Thursday. Can't wait to get there!
   Love, Ben
2. Tuesday
3. lazy
4. August
5. locked
6. pen
7. note

Page 77
1. Central
2. Alaska
3. west
4. 3:05 (five after three)
5. 4:45 (quarter to five)

Page 78
1. "I hope she doesn't break my new car," said Nick.
2. We saw Mary's cat running down Washington Street.
3. (c)rowd, (k)eeper, ra(ck), (c)ost
4. de(c)ide, (s)enten(c)e, ki(ss), co(s)t
5. construct

6. hazardous

Page 79
1. Denver
2. Atlantic Ocean
3. 1/2, 1/3, 1/2, 1/4

Page 80
1. Jerry and I aren't going to New York in February.
2. Mr. Baker said we have to draw a map of Canada.
3. hear, can't, rubbing
4. what happened
5. carried
6. stood

Page 81
1. Nashville
2. California
3. North America
4. 1:30
5. 11:25 (twenty-five after 11)
6. 12:50 (ten to one)

Page 82
1. "Lisa gave me a turtle named Shelly," said Megan.
2. Dr. Judy James took out my tonsils.
3. why-shy, near-neat
4. ought-thoughtful, are-careless
5. a naming word
6. Jenny, Nicole

Page 83
1. Southern U.S.
2. Louisiana
3. Superior
4. Kate
5. Lisa
6. 7

Page 84
1. Grandpa Peterson will be here by 12:30. Will you be home then?
2. "Can I take my new puppy to school?" asked Donald.
3. hug
4. stir
5. grab
6. fat

7. raise
8. happy
9. fear

Page 85
1. Ohio River
2. Idaho
3. True
4. 1:50 (ten to two)
5. 2:05 (five after two)

Page 86
1. That book isn't on the shelf like Roger said it was.
2. We don't have any maps of China.
3. polite, grab, decided
4. not happy
5. full of beauty
6. can use again
7. can't be used

Page 87
1. Missouri River
2. New York
3. Arizona
4. 1 pint
5. 1 quart
6. 8 pints

Page 88
1. We're moving to a new house. The address is 9824 Winding Road, Tulsa, Oklahoma.
2. "Will you please let me go to the corner alone?" asked Megan.
3. earth
4. teach
5. friend
6. wild
7. straight
8. sick
9. light

Page 89
1. Alabama, Georgia
2. Great Lakes
3. scale
4. clock
5. ruler or measuring tape

110   *Wake Up, Brain!!* • Grade 3   ECS Learning Systems, Inc.

Answer Key

Page 90
1. My homework tonight is page 32 for math, Chapter 13 for geography, and reading <u>Jimmy and the Boa Constrictor</u>.
2. Karen said she took her piano lessons on Tuesdays.
3. old
4. right
5. everybody or anybody
6. The sandwich ate the chips. /Wiley Coyote was hit by a truck and got right back up.

Page 91
1. eastern
2. Africa
3. Cuba
4. 3 sides and 3 angles
5. 4 sides and 4 angles
6. triangle

Page 92
1. My mom grew tulips, daffodils, roses, and weeds in her garden.
2. For Thanksgiving I wrote a poem called "Mr. Turkey and the Pilgrims."
3. K
4. S
5. K
6. !
7. ?
8. .

Page 93
1. Hawaii
2. True
3. False
4. 89 – 19 = 70
5. 92 – 73 = 19

Page 94
1. There wasn't a single crayon left in the box.
2. I'm sure that John was hit on the head.
3. owl, elf, oven, egg
4. but he don't have time.
5. Me and Mom let my little brother

Page 95
1. east
2. Rio Grande
3. 95¢
4. 73¢
5. $2.01

Page 96
1. Darla took her ballet lesson every Thursday.
2. Aunt Jenny invited us to her house for Christmas Eve dinner.
3. Ki(ss), carele(ss), i(c)e, co(s)t, fier(c)e
4. Bla(ck), po(k)e, (c)oo(k), (k)ite, ca(k)e, (c)ool
5. Varied answers.
6. Varied answers.
7. Varied answers.

Page 97
1. South America
2. Asia, Europe, and North America
3. True
4. 54
5. 60
6. 5

Page 98
1. Mom bought me a book called <u>Tom Swift and the Forest Fire</u>.
2. Aunt Ruby gave Jake and me an electric train for our birthday.
3. (F)uzzy, (ph)one, i(f), enou(gh), (f)rankly, tou(gh)
4. (J)unk, ple(dg)e, a(g)e, (j)u(dg)e
5. my brother
6. woke up
7. this morning

Page 99
1. No
2. Florida
3. Small hand on 7, big hand on 6.
4. Small hand on 9, big hand on 3.
5. Small hand on 1, big hand on 9.
6. Small hand on 3, big hand on 2.

Page 100
1. My lunch tray slid off the table.
2. We haven't any candy./We have no candy.
3. seeds, fruit
4. Appropriate verb (e.g., ran)
5. Appropriate verb (e.g., eats)
6. Appropriate verb (e.g., went)

Page 101
1. map
2. lake
3. 1½ inches
4. 2 inches
5. 1 inch

Page 102
1. Yesterday was my appointment with Dr. Johnson.
2. Where have you been?
3. grass
4. house
5. together
6. there or they're
7. board
8. hair
9. ate

Page 103
1. The compass should indicate N, S, E, W correctly.
2. 121
3. 274
4. 48

Page 104
1. We were going to the library, but we changed our minds.
2. What is the best way to travel to Hawaii?
3. grade, grain, grant, grasp, grass, gray
4. On July, New, Hampshire, Christa McAuliffe, Americans, America's

Page 105
1. California, Maine, Texas, Idaho
2. 3 of 4 are colored in.
3. 1 of 2 are colored in.
4. 2 of 3 are colored in.

ECS Learning Systems, Inc.   *Wake Up, Brain!!* • Grade 3

About the Authors

After graduating from the University of Utah, **Michelle Ball** (right) lived in Salt Lake City before returning to her hometown of Idaho Falls, Idaho. She has three children, Conrad, Rebecca, and Patrick. Her husband, Doug, is a great support in her life and has always valued her love for teaching. He is an active part of her school life and known in the neighborhood as "Mrs. Ball's Husband."

Michelle's 15 years of teaching experiences in kindergarten, second, and third grades provided a sound foundation for her current position as a teacher in a multi-age classroom. "Teaching three grades at once has definitely enhanced my life (my dear friend and co-author's daughter was my student). Working in a multi-age classroom has provided opportunities to develop organizational skills and teaching strategies that benefit my students. Working with children has given me countless joys. My students have enriched my life beyond measure."

Barbara Morris (left) grew up and received her education in Idaho. A career in banking took her to Utah and California before she and her husband, Tony, became parents and moved back "home" to Idaho to raise their only child, Jennifer. As a new parent, "Barb" developed her own publishing skills and eventually built a small, in-home desktop publishing business.

Barb met Michelle as she enrolled Jennifer in Michelle's multi-grade classroom. Eventually, their relationship developed into a bond of friendship that enhanced both lives and fulfilled their individual goals and dreams. As a full-time office manager for a local hospital, Barb had little time to volunteer in the classroom, but had a desire to stay involved with her child's education. She offered her desktop publishing skills to Michelle, who sketched out student worksheets, literature studies, and classroom management tools. Barb converted them into the original student-friendly and teacher-helpful *Wake Up, Brain!!*, which developed into the new series for grades 1 through 6.

ECS Learning Systems, Inc.